Sainsbury's

·RECIPE·LIBRARY·

VEGETARIAN SUPPERS

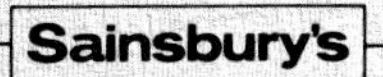

·RECIPE·LIBRARY·

VEGETARIAN SUPPERS

Jane Suthering

CONTENTS

Published exclusively for J Sainsbury plc
Stamford House Stamford Street London SE1 9LL
by Martin Books
Simon & Schuster International Group
Fitzwilliam House 32 Trumpington Street Cambridge CB2 1QY

ISBN 0 85941 543 0
First published 1987
Third impression 1990

Printed and bound in Italy by Arnoldo Mondadori Editore

INTRODUCTION

More and more people are eating vegetarian meals than ever before. Some say it is for health reasons, others because vegetables are less expensive than meat or fish and can provide just as good nourishment. Some people simply prefer the flavour of vegetarian dishes. Whatever the reason, there is a wealth of vegetables available to us and *Vegetarian Suppers* offers delicious ideas for preparing them.

The main course dishes are intended to be served with simple vegetables or salads as complete meals. I have also provided recipes for vegetable accompaniments and a few starter ideas if you wish to serve a more elaborate meal. For a light supper you could serve several of these accompaniments together, rather in the oriental style.

There is a large salad section and I suggest that you serve three or four together as a complete supper. Always include a variety of textures and colours and ensure that some of the salads contain protein foods—such as beans, cheese or eggs—although any meal may be supplemented by adding such ingredients. The suppertime soups can be served as a meal in themselves, especially if served with bread and cheese, or a salad.

Vegetable stock is used in most of the cooked dishes. Vegetable stock cubes are available for emergencies or to add extra flavour to a made stock, but do always keep vegetable cooking water and supplement the flavour with vegetable or yeast extract—there are several very good extracts, based on sea vegetables, available now. The addition of finely ground nuts, such as walnuts, can also enhance flavour and improve food value.

Vegetarian dishes can provide endless variety so don't let your cooking stop at cauliflower cheese!

NOTES

Ingredients are given in both metric and imperial measures. Use either set of quantities but not a mixture of both in any one recipe.

All spoon measurements are level:
1 tablespoon = one 15 ml spoon
1 teaspoon = one 5 ml spoon.

Ovens should be preheated to the temperature specified.

Freshly ground black pepper is intended where pepper is listed.

Fresh herbs are used unless otherwise stated. If unobtainable dried herbs can be substituted in cooked dishes but halve the quantities.

Eggs are standard size 3 unless otherwise stated.

Strict vegetarians can use vegetarian cheeses, made with non-animal rennet, where cheese is specified. Use vegetarian cheddar unless a soft cheese is listed in which case curd cheese or skimmed milk soft cheese is more suitable.

MOZZARELLA AND TOMATO SKEWERS

8 slices French bread, 1 cm (½ inch) thick, quartered
5 tablespoons olive oil
250 g (8 oz) Mozzarella cheese, cut into 24 even-sized pieces
24 cherry tomatoes
4 tablespoons chopped mixed herbs (including parsley, chives, basil, oregano or marjoram)
salt and pepper to taste
salad leaves to garnish

Serves 4
Preparation time:
25 minutes
Cooking time:
3–4 minutes
Freezing:
Not recommended

1. Sprinkle the bread evenly with the oil, then season with salt and pepper.
2. Onto each of 8 small skewers, tightly thread alternately 4 pieces of bread, 3 pieces of cheese and 3 tomatoes, starting and finishing with bread.
3. Arrange on a heatproof dish, season generously with salt and pepper and sprinkle with the herbs.
4. Place under a preheated hot grill for 3–4 minutes, until the bread is golden and the cheese is beginning to melt. Serve immediately, garnished with salad leaves.

CAPONATA

625 g (1¼ lb) aubergines, diced
2 tablespoons olive oil
1 onion, chopped
4 celery sticks, chopped
2 cloves garlic, chopped
397 g (14 oz) can chopped tomatoes
125 g (4 oz) tomato purée
50 g (2 oz) pitted black olives, chopped
2 tablespoons capers
1 tablespoon red wine vinegar
salt and pepper to taste
celery leaves to garnish

Serves 4–6
Preparation time:
20 minutes
Cooking time:
25–30 minutes
Freezing:
Recommended

1. Sprinkle the aubergines with salt and set aside.
2. Heat the oil in a pan, add the onion, celery and garlic and sauté for 10 minutes.
3. Pour boiling water over the aubergines; drain well. Add to the pan and cook for 10 minutes, stirring frequently.
4. Add the tomatoes and tomato purée and simmer for 5–10 minutes, until most of the liquid has evaporated.
5. Leave until cold, then stir in the remaining ingredients. Garnish with celery leaves and serve with warm pitta bread, cut into fingers.

OKRA BHAJI

An Indian influence of spice makes these okra—sometimes known as ladies fingers—quite delicious.

2 tablespoons oil
½ teaspoon cumin seeds
½ teaspoon turmeric
1 onion, chopped finely
1 green chilli, slit lengthways
500 g (1 lb) okra, halved lengthways
1 teaspoon sugar
4 tomatoes, chopped
4 tablespoons lemon juice
salt to taste

Serves 4
Preparation time: About 15 minutes
Cooking time: 10–15 minutes
Freezing: Not recommended

1. Heat the oil in a pan, add the cumin seeds, turmeric, onion and chilli and cook until the onion is transparent. Add the okra and sauté for 5–7 minutes, until just tender.
2. Add the sugar, tomatoes and lemon juice and simmer for 3–5 minutes. Season with salt. Serve hot.

BEETROOT FRITTERS WITH ORANGE SAUCE

An unusual yet delicious way to serve beetroot—hot with a crisp golden coating.

50 g (2 oz) plain flour
1 teaspoon dried tarragon
5 tablespoons lager
1 egg white, whisked stiffly
500 g (1 lb) beetroot, cooked and cut into bite-size pieces
salt and pepper to taste
oil for deep-frying
FOR THE SAUCE:
5 tablespoons each natural yogurt and soured cream
grated rind of 1 small orange
1 tablespoon each chopped parsley and chives
TO GARNISH:
chives and parsley sprigs

Serves 4
Preparation time: 20 minutes
Cooking time: About 5 minutes per batch
Freezing: Not recommended

1. Mix together the flour, tarragon, lager, and salt and pepper until smooth, then fold in the egg white.
2. Dip each piece of beetroot in the batter, then deep-fry in batches in hot oil until crisp and golden. Drain on kitchen paper and keep warm.
3. To make the sauce, mix all the ingredients together, seasoning with salt and pepper.
4. Serve the beetroot hot, garnished with chives and parsley, and accompanied by the orange sauce.

TAPENADE AND GOATS' CHEESE CROÛTES

50 g (2 oz) pitted black olives
1 tablespoon capers
15 g (½ oz) onion
1 teaspoon French mustard
1 tablespoon chopped parsley
2 teaspoons Mayonnaise
12 slices French bread, 1 cm (½ inch) thick
125 g (4 oz) goats' cheese, cut into 12 slices
50 g (2 oz) mixed salad leaves
2 tablespoons French Dressing (page 70)
paprika to garnish

Serves 4
Preparation time: 20 minutes
Cooking time: 3–4 minutes
Freezing: Not recommended

1. Place the olives, capers, onion, mustard, parsley and mayonnaise in a food processor and work until smooth.
2. Toast the French bread until golden on both sides, then spread each piece with a little olive mixture and top with a slice of cheese. Cook under a preheated hot grill until the cheese is just melting.
3. Toss the salad leaves in the dressing and arrange on 4 individual plates. Arrange the croûtes beside the salad and sprinkle with paprika. Serve immediately.

MUSHROOM CAPS WITH BUCKWHEAT

If you cannot buy buckwheat, use bulgar wheat instead.

125 g (4 oz) buckwheat
1 egg, beaten
300 ml (½ pint) vegetable stock
2 cloves garlic, crushed
4 large flat mushrooms
3 tablespoons chopped parsley
2 tablespoons dry sherry
50 g (2 oz) Parmesan cheese, grated
salt and pepper to taste

Serves 4
Preparation time: 30 minutes
Cooking time: 15–20 minutes
Freezing: Not recommended

1. Mix the buckwheat with the beaten egg and fry without any fat until dry and golden. Add the stock and garlic, cover and bring to the boil, then simmer for 15 minutes, until the buckwheat is tender. Remove the lid and bubble rapidly until no free liquid remains.
2. Remove the mushroom stalks and chop finely. Add to the buckwheat with the remaining ingredients.
3. Pile the mixture on top of the mushroom caps and place in an ovenproof dish. Cover and cook in a preheated oven, 200°C/400°F/Gas Mark 6, for 15–20 minutes, until the mushrooms are tender. Serve with Greek yogurt.

CARROT RAGOÛT

2 tablespoons oil
15 g (½ oz) butter
350 g (12 oz) small onions
350 g (12 oz) button mushrooms
750 g (1½ lb) carrots, cut into chunks the same size as the onions
50 g (2 oz) raisins
150 ml (¼ pint) dry white wine
150 ml (¼ pint) vegetable stock
1 teaspoon caraway seeds
1 tablespoon cornflour blended with 2 tablespoons water
salt and pepper to taste

Serves 4
Preparation time: 20 minutes
Cooking time: 30 minutes
Freezing: Recommended

1. Heat the oil and butter in a large pan, add the onions and sauté until golden. Add the mushrooms and cook quickly, stirring, for 1 minute. Add the carrots, raisins, wine, stock and caraway seeds. Bring to the boil, then cover and simmer for 30 minutes or until the carrots are just tender.
2. Stir in the blended cornflour and cook, stirring, until thickened. Season with salt and pepper.
3. Serve with jacket or new potatoes and salad.

SWEET POTATO CUTLETS

750 g (1½ lb) sweet potatoes, chopped
1 tablespoon oil
1 clove garlic, chopped finely
1 onion, chopped finely
1 teaspoon curry powder
2 tablespoons mango chutney
pinch of grated nutmeg
1 egg, beaten
75 g (3 oz) flaked almonds
salt and pepper to taste
oil for shallow-frying

Serves 4
Preparation time: About 30 minutes
Cooking time: 10 minutes
Freezing: Recommended

1. Steam or cook the sweet potatoes in boiling salted water for 15–20 minutes, until tender. Drain well, then mash.
2. Heat the oil in a pan, add the garlic, onion and curry powder and sauté until softened. Add to the potato with the chutney, nutmeg, and salt and pepper.
3. Shape the mixture into 4 'cutlets', dip in the beaten egg and cover with the flaked almonds.
4. Shallow-fry in hot oil for 5 minutes on each side until golden brown. Serve with a tomato and orange salad.

AUBERGINE AND BEAN LAYER BAKE

1 kg (2 lb) aubergines, sliced
2 tablespoons oil
1 onion, chopped finely
2 cloves garlic, chopped
800 g (1 lb 12 oz) can peeled tomatoes
2 bay leaves
2 teaspoons dried oregano
400 g (14 oz) can white kidney beans, drained
250 g (8 oz) Mozzarella cheese, sliced
50 g (2 oz) Parmesan cheese, grated
50 g (2 oz) fresh breadcrumbs
salt and pepper to taste

Serves 4–6
Preparation time: 45 minutes
Cooking time: 45 minutes
Freezing: Recommended

1. Sprinkle the aubergines with salt and set aside.
2. Heat the oil in a pan, add the onion and garlic and sauté until golden. Add the tomatoes with their juice, bay leaves and oregano and simmer for about 25 minutes, until thickened. Season with salt and pepper.
3. Rinse the aubergines well, then cook in boiling water for about 5 minutes, until tender. Drain well.
4. Arrange a layer of aubergines in a large ovenproof dish, cover with tomato sauce, then a layer of beans, then Mozzarella cheese. Repeat the layers, finishing with aubergine.
5. Sprinkle with the Parmesan cheese and breadcrumbs and cook in a preheated oven, 190°C/375°F/Gas Mark 5, for 45 minutes, until bubbling and crisp. Serve hot.

CAULIFLOWER, PEAR AND PEPPER PIE

An unusual combination of fruit, vegetable and cheese topped with a walnut pastry.

350 g (12 oz) cauliflower florets
25 g (1 oz) butter
1 onion, diced
1 red pepper, cored, seeded and diced
25 g (1 oz) plain flour
150 ml (1/4 pint) milk (approximately)
2 ripe pears, diced
125 g (4 oz) red Leicester cheese, grated
pinch of mustard powder
salt and pepper to taste
FOR THE PASTRY:
125 g (4 oz) self-raising wholemeal flour
125 g (4 oz) self-raising white flour, sifted
50 g (2 oz) walnuts, ground
50 g (2 oz) butter
2 tablespoons oil
4 tablespoons cold water

1. Cook the cauliflower florets in a minimum of water for 5–7 minutes, until just tender. Drain well, reserving the liquid, and chop roughly.
2. Melt the butter in a pan, add the onion and red pepper and sauté until the onion is transparent. Stir in the flour and cook for 1–2 minutes, stirring.
3. Make up the reserved liquid to 300 ml (½ pint) with milk, then add to the pan, stirring until thickened.
4. Add the remaining ingredients, then transfer to a 1.2 litre (2 pint) pie dish.
5. To make the pastry, mix the dry ingredients together, rub in the butter until the mixture resembles breadcrumbs, then add the oil and water to make a firm dough. Roll out on a lightly floured surface and use to cover the dish. Crimp the edges well and make a slit in the centre.
6. Bake in a preheated oven, 200°C/400°F/Gas Mark 6, for 30 minutes, until golden. Serve hot.

Serves 4
Preparation time:
35–40 minutes
Cooking time:
30 minutes
Freezing:
Recommended

KITCHERI

175 g (6 oz) Basmati rice
175 g (6 oz) red lentils
25 g (1 oz) butter
2 tablespoons oil
1 large onion, sliced
2 cloves garlic, crushed
250 g (8 oz) carrots, cut into sticks
1 teaspoon ground cumin
2 bay leaves
2 × 5 cm (2 inch) pieces cinnamon stick
8 cloves
8 cardamom pods, bruised
600 ml (1 pint) vegetable stock
1 ripe avocado, diced
2 large tomatoes, diced
salt and pepper to taste

Serves 4
Preparation time:
25–30 minutes
Cooking time:
30 minutes
Freezing:
Recommended at end of stage 3

1. Soak the rice and lentils in cold water.
2. Heat the butter and oil in a pan, add the onion, garlic and carrots and sauté for 10 minutes. Add the cumin, bay leaves, cinnamon, cloves and cardamom pods. Drain the rice and lentils, add to the pan and cook for 5 minutes.
3. Add the stock, bring to the boil, then cover and simmer for 15 minutes.
4. Stir in the avocado, tomatoes, and salt and pepper and serve immediately, with a side salad.

GREEN SPRING FRAZE

A quick, colourful and nutritious meal for one.

2 eggs
1 tablespoon chopped mixed herbs, e.g. dill, mint, parsley, chervil
50 g (2 oz) cottage cheese
15 g (½ oz) butter
6 spring onions, sliced thickly
50 g (2 oz) crisp lettuce, shredded
50 g (2 oz) mangetouts, sliced lengthways, or cooked peas
salt and pepper to taste

Serves 1
Preparation time:
10 minutes
Cooking time:
About 8 minutes
Freezing:
Not recommended

1. Beat together the eggs, herbs, and salt and pepper, then stir in the cottage cheese.
2. Melt the butter in an 18 cm (7 inch) omelette pan, add the spring onions, lettuce and mangetouts or peas and sauté for 1 minute.
3. Pour in the egg mixture immediately and stir over a high heat until lightly set. Reduce heat to low, cover the pan with a plate and leave to set for 5 minutes.
4. Serve immediately, with a tomato salad.

VEGETABLE PAELLA

Based on the classic Spanish paella, but using an interesting mixture of vegetables instead of fish.

4 tablespoons oil
2 cloves garlic, crushed
1 large onion, sliced
4 celery sticks, sliced
1 teaspoon paprika
1 each red, green and yellow pepper, cored, seeded and cut into squares
125 g (4 oz) whole green beans
350 g (12 oz) Italian risotto rice
397 g (14 oz) can peeled tomatoes
2 pinches saffron strands
900 ml (1½ pints) vegetable stock
400 g (14 oz) can artichoke hearts, drained and halved
125 g (4 oz) frozen peas
50 g (2 oz) pitted black olives
1 tablespoon lemon juice
2 tablespoons chopped parsley
salt and pepper to taste
lemon wedges and parsley to garnish

Serves 4
Preparation time: 20 minutes
Cooking time: 25–30 minutes
Freezing: Recommended

1. Heat the oil in a pan, add the garlic, onion and celery and sauté until the onion is transparent. Add the paprika, peppers and beans and sauté for 2–3 minutes. Add the rice and cook for 2 minutes, stirring constantly.
2. Add the tomatoes with their juice, saffron and stock and simmer gently for 15–20 minutes, stirring frequently, until almost all the liquid has been absorbed.
3. Add the remaining ingredients and heat gently for about 5 minutes. Garnish with lemon wedges and parsley to serve.

CABBAGE AND CHILLI TIMBALE

1 tablespoon oil
1 onion, chopped
1 large red pepper, cored, seeded and chopped
1 small green chilli, chopped finely
½ teaspoon ground cumin
1 teaspoon dried oregano
75 g (3 oz) long-grain rice
397 g (14 oz) can peeled tomatoes
150 ml (¼ pint) vegetable stock
432 g (15¼ oz) can red kidney beans, drained
125 g (4 oz) Cheddar cheese, grated
1 Savoy cabbage, weighing about 500 g (1 lb), separated into leaves
salt and pepper to taste

1. Heat the oil in a pan, add the onion, red pepper and chilli and sauté for 5 minutes. Add the cumin, oregano and rice and cook for 1–2 minutes, stirring.
2. Add the tomatoes with their juice and stock. Simmer, uncovered, for 20 minutes, until the liquid is completely absorbed and the rice cooked.
3. Stir in the kidney beans, cheese, and salt and pepper and leave to cool.
4. Blanch the cabbage leaves in boiling water for 2 minutes, until just tender. Drain and dry well, then remove the coarse central stems.
5. Lightly grease a 1.2 litre (2 pint) pudding basin or a 20 cm (8 inch) cake tin and line with some of the larger leaves. Set aside 3–4 large leaves to cover the top.
6. Fill the basin or tin with alternate layers of rice mixture and leaves, pressing down well. Finish with the reserved leaves, cover with greased foil and cook in a preheated oven, 180°C/350°F/Gas Mark 4, for 30 minutes for the tin or 45 minutes for the basin, until heated through.
7. Serve on a warmed serving plate with natural yogurt or soured cream sprinkled with chives, and potatoes.

Serves 4
Preparation time:
1 hour
Cooking time:
30–45 minutes
Freezing:
Recommended

FETA AND COURGETTE TRIANGLES

350 g (12 oz) fillo pastry (12 sheets)
75 g (3 oz) butter, melted
250 g (8 oz) courgettes, grated coarsely
125 g (4 oz) cooking apple, peeled, cored and grated coarsely
200 g (7 oz) packet Feta cheese, crumbled
2 spring onions, sliced thinly
2 tablespoons chopped mint
pepper to taste

Serves 4
Preparation time: 30–35 minutes
Cooking time: 15 minutes
Freezing: Recommended

1. Halve the sheets of pastry lengthways, then divide into 8 piles, brushing each pile generously with butter.
2. Place the courgettes and apple on a clean tea towel, wrap and 'wring out', squeezing out as much moisture as possible. Mix with the remaining ingredients, adding pepper to taste.
3. Place one eighth of the mixture 2.5 cm (1 inch) in from one short side of each pile of pastry. Fold one of the adjacent corners diagonally over the filling to the opposite side to make a triangle at one end of the strip. Continue folding this triangle over and over until all the pastry strip is wrapped around the triangle. Place on a baking sheet.
4. Brush the parcels with the remaining butter, then bake in a preheated oven, 200°C/400°F/Gas Mark 6, for 15 minutes, until golden brown. Serve with a tomato salad.

MUSHROOM AND BARLEY BAKE

175 g (6 oz) pearl or pot barley, washed thoroughly
25 g (1 oz) butter
1 onion, chopped
6 celery sticks, sliced
250 g (8 oz) mushrooms, sliced
1 vegetable stock cube, crumbled
1 tablespoon cornflour
300 ml (½ pint) milk
4 tomatoes, sliced
salt and pepper to taste
chopped herbs to garnish

1. Place the barley in a measuring jug and add water to reach the 600 ml (1 pint) mark. Leave to soak in a cool place for at least 4 hours, or overnight.
2. Melt the butter in a pan, add the onion and celery and sauté until the onion is transparent. Add the mushrooms and sauté for 1–2 minutes. Add the barley with its liquid and the stock cube. Cover and simmer for 30–45 minutes, until tender.
3. Blend the cornflour with a little of the milk, then add to the barley with the remaining milk. Heat gently, stirring, until thickened and creamy. Season with salt and pepper.
4. Transfer to a heatproof serving dish. Arrange the tomatoes on top, then place under a preheated hot grill until lightly browned. Sprinkle with the herbs and serve with crisp green vegetables.

Serves 4
Preparation time: 15 minutes, plus soaking time
Cooking time: 30–45 minutes
Freezing: Recommended

BEAN AND VEGETABLE STEW WITH HERB DUMPLINGS

2 tablespoons oil
2 cloves garlic, chopped
500 g (1 lb) leeks, sliced
1 large carrot, diced
250 g (8 oz) mushrooms, sliced
397 g (14 oz) can tomatoes
300 ml (½ pint) vegetable stock
1 tablespoon paprika
1 tablespoon soy sauce
432 g (15¼ oz) can red kidney beans, drained
salt and pepper to taste
FOR THE DUMPLINGS:
125 g (4 oz) self-raising flour, sifted
50 g (2 oz) vegetable suet
3 tablespoons chopped mixed herbs
5 tablespoons cold water

Serves 4
Preparation time:
40 minutes
Cooking time:
40 minutes
Freezing:
Recommended

1. Heat the oil in a pan, add the garlic, leeks, carrot, and mushrooms and sauté until just tender.
2. Add the tomatoes with their juice, stock, paprika and soy sauce. Bring to the boil, then cover and simmer for 20 minutes.
3. Meanwhile, make the dumplings. Mix all the ingredients together to give a firm dough, then shape into 12 balls.
4. Add the kidney beans, and salt and pepper to the stew. Arrange the dumplings on top, cover and simmer for 20 minutes, until the dumplings are light and fluffy. Serve as soon as possible.

FARMHOUSE ONIONS

The traditional combination of sage, onion and cheese goes well with the red wine gravy.

4 Spanish onions
1 tablespoon oil
15 g (½ oz) butter
125 g (4 oz) mushrooms, chopped
50 g (2 oz) mixed nuts, chopped
50 g (2 oz) fresh breadcrumbs
4 tablespoons vegetable stock
1 tablespoon chopped sage
125 g (4 oz) Cheddar cheese, grated
FOR THE RED WINE GRAVY:
25 g (1 oz) butter
25 g (1 oz) shallot or onion, chopped finely
2 tablespoons plain flour
150 ml (¼ pint) vegetable stock
150 ml (¼ pint) red wine
2 tablespoons chopped parsley
salt and pepper to taste

1. Cook the onions in their skins in boiling water for about 20 minutes, until just tender. Leave to cool.
2. Cut the onions in half, starting at the root end but leaving them intact at the stalk end. Scoop out the flesh, leaving a 1 cm (½ inch) shell. Chop the onion flesh.
3. Heat the oil and butter in a pan, add the chopped onions and mushrooms and sauté until golden. Add the nuts, breadcrumbs, stock and sage and mix well. Remove from the heat and add the cheese, and salt and pepper.
4. Spoon the mixture into the onion skins and cook in a preheated oven, 200°C/400°F/Gas Mark 6, for 15–20 minutes, until bubbling and golden.
5. Meanwhile, make the red wine gravy. Melt the butter in a pan, add the shallot or onion and sauté until golden. Stir in the flour and cook until browned. Add the stock and wine, stirring until thickened, then simmer for 1–2 minutes. Add salt and pepper, and the parsley.
6. Serve the onions immediately, with the gravy and accompanied by broccoli and creamed potatoes.

Serves 4
Preparation time:
40 minutes
Cooking time:
15–20 minutes
Freezing:
Recommended

CALABRIAN PASTA

350 g (12 oz) broccoli
2 tablespoons oil
2 cloves garlic, sliced thinly
4 tablespoons pine nuts
4 tablespoons raisins
397 g (14 oz) can chopped tomatoes with herbs
350 g (12 oz) pasta shapes
salt and pepper to taste

Serves 4
Preparation time: 15 minutes
Cooking time: 10 minutes
Freezing: Not recommended

1. Peel the coarse skin from the broccoli stalks. Dice the stalks and cut the broccoli into small florets.
2. Heat the oil in a pan, add the garlic and sauté until golden. Add the pine nuts, raisins and tomatoes, bring to the boil, then simmer for 10 minutes.
3. Meanwhile, cook the pasta in boiling salted water according to packet instructions, until just tender.
4. At the same time cook the broccoli in a minimum of boiling water for 5 minutes, until just tender. Drain well.
5. Drain the pasta and combine with the tomato sauce and broccoli. Stir well, and season with salt and pepper. Heat through gently and serve immediately.

UPSIDE DOWN VEGETABLE SQUARES

2 tablespoons oil
1 clove garlic, crushed
1 onion, sliced
350 g (12 oz) courgettes, sliced
198 g (7 oz) can sweetcorn, drained
4 tomatoes, sliced
2 tablespoons chopped basil
salt and pepper to taste
FOR THE DOUGH:
75 g (3 oz) butter
250 g (8 oz) self-raising flour, sifted
6 tablespoons milk

Serves 6
Preparation time: 30 minutes
Cooking time: 20–25 minutes
Freezing: Recommended

1. Heat the oil in a pan, add the garlic, onion and courgettes and sauté until the onion is transparent. Add the remaining ingredients and stir well. Transfer to a 30 × 23 cm (12 × 9 inch) baking tin and leave to cool while making the dough.
2. Rub the butter into the flour until the mixture resembles breadcrumbs, stir in the milk and mix to a firm dough. Roll out on a lightly floured surface and use to cover the vegetable mixture, pressing down lightly.
3. Bake in a preheated oven, 200°C/400°F/Gas Mark 6, for 20–25 minutes, until golden brown.
4. Leave to cool slightly, then cut into 6 squares and turn out upside down onto a warmed serving dish.

GREEN AND WHITE FLORET GRATIN

A sophisticated variation of one of the most popular vegetable dishes ever known!

1 cauliflower, cut into florets
250 g (8 oz) broccoli, cut into florets
25 g (1 oz) butter
25 g (1 oz) plain flour
1 teaspoon coarse-grain mustard
300 ml (1/2 pint) milk
175 g (6 oz) matured Cheddar cheese, or half Cheddar and half Gruyère, grated
25 g (1 oz) walnut pieces
1 tablespoon sesame seeds
salt and pepper to taste

Serves 4
Preparation time: 15 minutes
Cooking time: 15 minutes
Freezing: Recommended

1. Cook the cauliflower and broccoli in boiling water for 5 minutes. Drain, reserving 150 ml (1/4 pint) of the cooking liquid, and keep warm.
2. Melt the butter in a small saucepan, stir in the flour and cook, stirring, for 1–2 minutes. Stir in the mustard and milk and bring to the boil, stirring constantly, until smooth.
3. Stir in three quarters of the cheese and the reserved liquid to give the sauce a coating consistency. Season with salt and pepper.
4. Arrange the vegetables in a heatproof serving dish, pour over the sauce, then sprinkle with the reserved cheese, walnuts and sesame seeds. Place under a preheated hot grill until golden brown.
5. Serve with creamed or jacket potatoes.

PARSNIP AND POTATO CAKES

500 g (1 lb) parsnips, chopped roughly
500 g (1 lb) potatoes, chopped roughly
1 tablespoon oil
1 small onion, chopped finely
2 tablespoons chopped parsley
1/2 teaspoon grated nutmeg
squeeze of lemon juice
salt and pepper to taste
oil for shallow-frying

FOR THE COATING:
50 g (2 oz) hazelnuts, shredded
25 g (1 oz) porridge oats
2 tablespoons chopped parsley

FOR THE SAUCE (OPTIONAL):
125 g (4 oz) redcurrants
125 ml (1/4 pint) vegetable stock
1 teaspoon arrowroot
3 tablespoons light brown soft sugar

1. Cook the parsnips and potatoes together in a minimum of boiling salted water for about 15 minutes, until tender. Drain well, then mash.
2. Heat the oil in a pan, add the onion and sauté until golden, then add to the parsnip mixture with the remaining ingredients. Mix well, then shape into 16 'cakes'.
3. Combine the coating ingredients and use to coat the 'cakes', pressing on firmly.
4. Heat a little oil in a frying pan and fry the 'cakes' in batches until golden on both sides. Place on a warmed serving dish and keep warm.
5. To make the sauce, if required, place all the ingredients in a small pan. Heat gently, stirring, until thickened, then simmer for 1–2 minutes. Season with salt and pepper.
6. Serve the parsnip and potato cakes with the sauce, mangetouts or peas and carrot sticks.

Serves 4
Preparation time:
30 minutes
Cooking time:
10–15 minutes per batch
Freezing:
Recommended

VEGETABLE KEBABS

Marinating the vegetables improves their flavour.

12 baby onions
250 g (8 oz) aubergine
250 g (8 oz) courgettes
1 red pepper, cored, seeded and cut into squares
12 button mushrooms
salt and pepper to taste
FOR THE MARINADE:
8 tablespoons oil
2 tablespoons lemon juice
2 tablespoons chopped mixed herbs
2 cloves garlic, crushed
1 teaspoon ground cumin
½ teaspoon ground ginger
¼ teaspoon turmeric
¼ teaspoon cayenne

Serves 4
Preparation time:
20 minutes, plus marinating
Cooking time:
About 5 minutes
Freezing:
Not recommended

1. Cook the onions in boiling water for 5 minutes; drain.
2. Cut the aubergine and courgettes into chunks.
3. Mix the marinade ingredients together in a large bowl, add all the vegetables and toss well. Leave for several hours, stirring occasionally.
4. Thread the vegetables onto 8 long skewers, season generously with salt and pepper and cook under a preheated moderate grill for about 5 minutes, turning once, until browned and tender. Serve immediately.

FENNEL GOULASH

Goulash is a rich paprika and tomato based stew—here fennel is the main ingredient.

3 bulbs fennel, weighing about 750 g (1½ lb)
2 tablespoons oil
1 large onion, sliced
2 tablespoons paprika
1 large red pepper, cored, seeded and diced
500 g (1 lb) potatoes, cut in 2.5 cm (1 inch) cubes
125 g (4 oz) mushrooms, sliced
1 tablespoon plain flour
397 g (14 oz) can chopped tomatoes
300 ml (½ pint) vegetable stock
salt and pepper to taste
natural yogurt to serve

Serves 4
Preparation time:
15 minutes
Cooking time:
About 30 minutes
Freezing:
Recommended

1. Cut the fennel stalks into 2.5 cm (1 inch) pieces, then quarter the bulbs.
2. Heat the oil in a pan, add the onion and paprika and sauté until softened. Add the remaining ingredients, bring to the boil, then cover and simmer for about 30 minutes, until the vegetables are tender.
3. Serve with the yogurt and hot garlic bread.

CASHEW NUT CURRY

50 g (2 oz) desiccated coconut
1 teaspoon coriander seeds
1 teaspoon poppy seeds
1 teaspoon ground cumin
½ teaspoon turmeric
¼ teaspoon chilli powder
2 tablespoons oil
6 celery sticks, sliced
2 onions, sliced
250 g (8 oz) unsalted cashews, broken
300 ml (½ pint) vegetable stock
4 tomatoes, skinned and chopped
salt and pepper to taste
FOR THE MANGO RAITA:
1 large ripe mango
150 g (5.3 oz) carton natural set yogurt
1 spring onion, sliced
1 teaspoon cumin seeds, roasted
TO GARNISH:
shredded coriander leaves

Serves 4
Preparation time: 25 minutes
Cooking time: 30 minutes
Freezing: Not recommended

1. Grind the coconut, coriander and poppy seeds, cumin, turmeric and chilli powder together in a coffee grinder. Alternatively, use an electric blender, adding 1 tablespoon of the oil.
2. Heat the oil in a pan, add the celery and onions and sauté for 5 minutes, until lightly coloured. Add the ground spices and cashews and cook for 5 minutes, stirring frequently. Add the stock and bring to the boil. Add the tomatoes, cover and simmer for 30 minutes. Season with salt and pepper.
3. Meanwhile, prepare the mango raita. Cut the mango either side of the stone, scoop out all the flesh and chop. Mix with the remaining ingredients.
4. Sprinkle the curry with shredded coriander and serve with the raita.

PARMESAN PUDDINGS

125 g (4 oz) plain flour
1 egg
150 ml (¼ pint) milk
150 ml (¼ pint) water
25 g (1 oz) Parmesan or other strong flavoured cheese, grated
15 g (½ oz) white vegetable fat
FOR THE FILLING:
1 tablespoon oil
15 g (½ oz) butter
1 onion, chopped finely
750 g (1½ lb) root vegetables, including carrot, turnip, swede and parsnips, grated finely
2 tablespoons grated horseradish
salt and pepper to taste

1. Sift the flour into a bowl, add the egg, milk and water and whisk to a batter. Season generously with salt and pepper and stir in the cheese.
2. Dot 8 individual Yorkshire pudding tins with a little white fat. Place in a preheated oven, 230°C/450°F/Gas Mark 8, until the fat has melted, then pour in the batter. Bake for 15–20 minutes, until risen and golden.
3. Meanwhile, prepare the filling. Heat the oil and butter in a pan, add the onion and sauté until golden. Add the grated vegetables and cook until just tender, stirring frequently. Stir in the horseradish, and salt and pepper.
4. Remove the puddings from their tins and pile the vegetable mixture into the centre. Serve immediately with red wine gravy (see page 22) if you wish.

Serves 4
Preparation time:
25 minutes
Cooking time:
15–20 minutes
Freezing:
Not recommended

VEGETABLE TEMPURA

125 g (4 oz) each courgettes, mangetouts, baby sweetcorn
4 small red onions, each weighing 25 g (1 oz)
1 large red pepper, cored and seeded
oil for deep-frying
light soy sauce to serve

FOR THE TEMPURA BATTER:
125 g (4 oz) rice flour
75 g (3 oz) plain flour
4 teaspoons baking powder
1 tablespoon mustard powder
2 teaspoons semolina
1 teaspoon salt
300–400 ml (1/2–2/3 pint) iced water

Serves 4
Preparation time: 30 minutes
Cooking time: 2–3 minutes per batch
Freezing: Not recommended

Illustrated opposite

1. Prepare all the vegetables: cut the courgettes into 5 mm (1/4 inch) slices, leave the mangetouts and sweetcorn whole, quarter the onions, and cut the red pepper into 2.5 cm (1 inch) pieces. Place on a clean tea towel or kitchen paper to absorb any moisture.
2. For the batter, sift the dry ingredients into a bowl, then beat in enough water to give a thin coating batter.
3. Dip the vegetables in the batter, remove with tongs or a fork when they are evenly coated, and drop straight into hot oil. Cook in batches for 2–3 minutes until crisp and golden brown. Drain on kitchen paper and keep warm.
4. Serve immediately, with light soy sauce.

STUFFED SQUASH RINGS

A moist nut and cottage cheese mixture makes a tasty filling. When in season, use marrow instead of squash.

1 butternut squash or marrow, weighing about 1 kg (2 lb)
600 ml (1 pint) vegetable stock
25 g (1 oz) butter
2 tablespoons oil
350 g (12 oz) onions, chopped
125 g (4 oz) mushrooms, chopped
50 g (2 oz) almonds, chopped
25 g (1 oz) desiccated coconut
125 g (4 oz) fresh breadcrumbs
4 tablespoons chopped herbs (including parsley, marjoram and thyme)
1 tablespoon tomato purée
227 g (8 oz) carton cottage cheese
dash of Tabasco
salt to taste

1. Cut the squash or marrow into 8 rounds and remove the seeds. Place in a single layer in a large shallow pan, add the stock and simmer for 10–15 minutes, until almost tender; cook in 2 batches, if necessary. Drain, reserving the stock, and set aside.
2. Meanwhile, heat the butter and oil in a pan, add the onions and sauté until light golden. Add the mushrooms and almonds and sauté for 5 minutes.
3. Remove from the heat, stir in the remaining ingredients and moisten with 8 tablespoons of the reserved stock.
4. Place the squash rings on a baking sheet and fill with the nut mixture. Cook in a preheated oven, 200°C/400°F/ Gas Mark 6, for 25 minutes, until tender. Serve hot.

Serves 4
Preparation time:
30 minutes
Cooking time:
About 25 minutes
Freezing:
Recommended

Illustrated on page 35

LENTIL AND CORIANDER CANNELLONI

The taste of fresh coriander is unmistakable. Parsley may be used instead, but the flavour will be quite different.

12 sheets lasagne
25 g (1 oz) Parmesan cheese, grated
FOR THE FILLING:
125 g (4 oz) onion
125 g (4 oz) carrot
2 celery sticks
1 tablespoon oil
2 cloves garlic, crushed
175 g (6 oz) red lentils
450 ml (3/4 pint) vegetable stock
1 teaspoon chopped thyme
150 g (5 oz) Mozzarella cheese, diced
113 g (4 oz) carton cottage cheese
50 g (2 oz) fresh wholemeal breadcrumbs
1 egg, beaten
3 tablespoons chopped coriander leaves
salt and pepper to taste
FOR THE TOMATO SAUCE:
800 g (1 lb 12 oz) can peeled tomatoes
1 teaspoon dried basil
FOR THE WHITE SAUCE:
25 g (1 oz) butter
25 g (1 oz) plain flour
300 ml (1/2 pint) milk
1 bay leaf
pinch of grated nutmeg

Serves 6
Preparation time:
About 1 hour
Cooking time:
40–45 minutes
Freezing:
Not recommended

1. For the filling, finely chop the vegetables. Heat the oil in a pan, add the vegetables and garlic and sauté for 5 minutes. Add the lentils, stock and thyme, bring to the boil, then cover and simmer for about 20 minutes, until the lentils are soft. Leave to cool.
2. Add half of the Mozzarella and all of the remaining filling ingredients. Stir well, then set aside.
3. To make the tomato sauce, place the tomatoes with their juice, basil, and salt and pepper in a pan. Stir to break up the tomatoes, then simmer for 15 minutes, until thickened. Set aside.
4. For the white sauce, melt the butter in a pan, stir in the flour and cook for 1–2 minutes, stirring. Gradually stir in the milk, then add the bay leaf and nutmeg. Simmer, stirring, for 2 minutes. Remove the bay leaf and season with salt and pepper. Set aside.
5. Cook the lasagne according to packet instructions, drain and lay flat on a work surface. Divide the filling between the sheets, roll up and place in a greased ovenproof serving dish. Top with the tomato sauce, then the white sauce, then sprinkle with the reserved Mozzarella and the Parmesan.
6. Cook in a preheated oven, 200°C/400°F/Gas Mark 6, for 40–45 minutes, until golden. Serve with a green salad.

Illustrated bottom right: Stuffed Squash Rings (see page 32)

CELERY, GRUYÈRE AND ALMOND BAKE

This can be made more substantial by baking in a pastry crust, if you wish.

1 large head celery, sliced into 2.5 cm (1 inch) lengths
300 ml (½ pint) vegetable stock
3 eggs
450 ml (¾ pint) milk
50 g (2 oz) ground almonds
25 g (1 oz) fresh white breadcrumbs
175 g (6 oz) Gruyère cheese, grated
good pinch of mustard powder
1 teaspoon paprika
25 g (1 oz) flaked almonds
salt and pepper to taste

Serves 4
Preparation time:
20 minutes
Cooking time:
About 1 hour
Freezing:
Not recommended

1. Cook the celery in the stock for about 15 minutes, until just tender. Drain thoroughly. (Reserve the stock for another recipe.)
2. Beat together the eggs and milk, then stir in the remaining ingredients, except the flaked almonds. Transfer to a buttered ovenproof dish and sprinkle with the almonds.
3. Place the dish in a roasting tin and pour in boiling water to come about halfway up the sides of the dish. Cook in a preheated oven, 160°C/325°F/Gas Mark 3, for about 1 hour, until set and golden.
4. Serve with new potatoes and baked tomatoes.

BRAZIL AND BULGAR WHEAT BURGERS

Use any nuts to vary these protein-packed burgers.

2 tablespoons oil
125 g (4 oz) onion, chopped finely
2 celery sticks, chopped finely
2 cloves garlic, crushed
125 g (4 oz) bulgar wheat
250 g (8 oz) brazil nuts, ground coarsely
300 ml (½ pint) vegetable stock
2 tablespoons tomato purée
2 tablespoons chopped parsley
2 teaspoons dried mixed herbs
1 egg (size 1), beaten
FOR THE ORANGE SAUCE:
25 g (1 oz) butter
25 g (1 oz) onion or shallot, chopped finely
1 tablespoon plain flour
150 ml (¼ pint) vegetable stock
grated rind and juice of 1 large orange
salt and pepper to taste

1. Heat the oil in a pan, add the onion, celery and garlic and sauté until soft. Add the bulgar wheat and nuts and sauté for a few minutes, until lightly golden. Add the stock and simmer until the liquid is absorbed.
2. Stir in the tomato purée, parsley, herbs and beaten egg, season generously with salt and pepper, and leave until cool enough to handle.
3. Shape into 4 oval 'burgers', place on a greased baking sheet and cook in a preheated oven, 200°C/400°F/Gas Mark 6, for 15–20 minutes, until heated through.
4. Meanwhile, make the orange sauce. Melt the butter in a pan, add the onion or shallot and sauté until golden. Add the flour and cook, stirring, for 1–2 minutes. Stir in the stock, orange rind and juice and simmer for 2–3 minutes. Season with salt and pepper.
5. Transfer the burgers to a warmed serving dish and accompany with the sauce and courgettes.

Serves 4
Preparation time: 20 minutes
Cooking time: 15–20 minutes
Freezing: Recommended

PEA AND GREEN PEPPERCORN SOUFFLÉ

Strictly halfway between a soufflé and a savoury pudding.

1–2 tablespoons dried breadcrumbs
350 g (12 oz) frozen peas
25 g (1 oz) butter
125 g (4 oz) spring onions, chopped
25 g (1 oz) plain flour
150 ml (¼ pint) milk
½ teaspoon green peppercorns
3 eggs, separated
2 tablespoons flaked almonds
salt to taste

Serves 4
Preparation time: 25 minutes
Cooking time: 45 minutes
Freezing: Not recommended

1. Lightly grease a 1.2 litre (2 pint) soufflé dish and coat the base and side with breadcrumbs. Shake out excess, then chill the dish.
2. Cook the peas in a minimum of boiling water until just tender. Drain well and set aside.
3. Melt the butter in a pan, add the spring onions and sauté lightly. Add the flour and cook for 1–2 minutes, stirring. Stir in the milk and bring to the boil, then simmer for 1–2 minutes. Cool slightly, then place in a food processor or blender. Add the peas and peppercorns and work together until smooth. Beat in the egg yolks.
4. Whisk the egg whites stiffly, with a generous pinch of salt, and fold into the pea purée. Transfer to the prepared dish, level the surface and sprinkle with the almonds.
5. Cook in a preheated oven, 180°C/350°F/Gas Mark 4, for 45 minutes. Serve immediately.

AUBERGINE PUFFS

Most unusual fritters—made by sandwiching cooked aubergine slices with a cheesy potato filling, then cooking in a light batter.

2 aubergines, total weight 500 g (1 lb), cut into 24 slices
250 g (8 oz) potatoes
50 g (2 oz) strong flavoured cheese, grated
600 ml (1 pint) tomato juice
2 cloves garlic, crushed
2 teaspoons grated fresh root ginger
salt and pepper to taste
oil for deep-frying
FOR THE BATTER:
1 egg
5–6 tablespoons milk
50 g (2 oz) plain flour, sifted

1. Sprinkle the aubergines with salt and set aside.

2. Steam or cook the potatoes in boiling salted water for 10–15 minutes, until tender. Drain well, mash, then mix in the cheese, and salt and pepper. Set aside.
3. Rinse the aubergines well, then place in a large shallow frying pan with the tomato juice, garlic and ginger. Bring to the boil, then cover and simmer for about 5 minutes, until tender. Drain well, reserving the juice.
4. Sandwich the aubergine slices together in pairs with the potato mixture.
5. To make the batter, whisk the egg and milk into the flour to give a coating consistency.
6. Heat the oil in a deep pan, dip the aubergine 'sandwiches' in the batter and deep-fry in batches until crisp and golden. Drain on kitchen paper. Reserve all the 'scraps' of batter.
7. Cook any remaining batter: pour it directly into the hot oil through the prongs of a fork and fry until crisp. Drain well.
8. Arrange the fritters on a warmed serving plate and top with the crispy batter 'scraps'.
9. Warm the reserved tomato juice and serve separately.

Serves 4
Preparation time:
35 minutes
Cooking time:
4–5 minutes per batch
Freezing:
Not recommended

MIXED VEGETABLE AND LENTIL CURRY

Lentils give substance and texture to the curry sauce, as well as adding extra protein.

250 g (8 oz) red lentils
4 tablespoons oil
1 large onion, sliced
2 large carrots, sliced
1 teaspoon turmeric
1 teaspoon cumin seeds
1 teaspoon chilli powder
1 teaspoon ground coriander
2 cloves garlic, crushed
250 g (8 oz) cauliflower florets
250 g (8 oz) courgettes, sliced
175 g (6 oz) okra
175 g (6 oz) tiny button mushrooms
4 tomatoes, skinned and quartered
salt to taste

Serves 4
Preparation time: 20 minutes
Cooking time: 35–40 minutes
Freezing: Recommended for up to 1 month

1. Place the lentils and 750 ml (1¼ pints) water in a pan, bring to the boil, then cover and simmer for 15 minutes.
2. Heat the oil in a large pan, add the onion and carrots and sauté for 5 minutes. Add all the spices and garlic and cook for 2 minutes, stirring constantly.
3. Add the cauliflower, courgettes, okra, mushrooms and lentils, cover and simmer for 10 minutes.
4. Stir in the tomatoes, season with salt, cover and simmer for 5–10 minutes, until the vegetables are just tender. Serve hot.

SPRING VEGETABLE CASSEROLE

25 g (1 oz) butter
250 g (8 oz) button onions
175 g (6 oz) carrots, cut into sticks
½ cucumber, halved lengthways, seeded and cut into 1 cm (½ inch) slices
1 small cauliflower, cut into florets
250 g (8 oz) tiny new potatoes
600 ml (1 pint) vegetable stock
125 g (4 oz) frozen peas or mange-touts
125 g (4 oz) crisp lettuce, shredded
grated rind and juice of ½ lemon
2 tablespoons shredded mint
1 egg yolk
142 ml (5 fl oz) carton single cream
2 tablespoons cornflour
salt and pepper to taste
mint sprigs to garnish

1. Melt the butter in a pan, add the onions, carrots and cucumber and sauté for 5 minutes. Add the cauliflower, potatoes and stock and bring to the boil, then cover and simmer for 10–15 minutes, until just tender.
2. Add the peas or mange-touts, lettuce, lemon rind and juice, and mint and simmer gently for 2–3 minutes.
3. Mix the egg yolk, cream and cornflour together, stir into the casserole and heat gently, stirring constantly, until thickened. Season with salt and pepper.
4. Serve garnished with mint and accompanied by rice.

Serves 4
Preparation time: 20 minutes
Cooking time: 20–25 minutes
Freezing: Not recommended

WINTER CRUMBLE BAKE

1.5 kg (3 lb) mixed root vegetables—including carrot, parsnip, kohlrabi, celeriac, potato, swede and turnip, sliced thickly
40 g (1½ oz) butter
1 onion, diced
40 g (1½ oz) plain flour
450 ml (¾ pint) milk
vegetable extract to taste
1 bay leaf
salt and pepper to taste

FOR THE CRUMBLE:
125 g (4 oz) plain flour, sifted
50 g (2 oz) porridge oats
50 g (2 oz) butter
25 g (1 oz) sunflower or pumpkin seeds
25 g (1 oz) flaked almonds or salted peanuts
4 tablespoons chopped parsley

TO GARNISH:
few bay leaves

Serves 6
Preparation time: 40 minutes
Cooking time: 30 minutes
Freezing: Recommended

1. Steam or cook the vegetables in boiling water for 15–20 minutes, until just tender. Drain well, reserving 300 ml (½ pint) of the cooking liquid.
2. Melt the butter in a pan, add the onion and sauté until transparent. Stir in the flour and cook for 1–2 minutes. Stir in the milk and reserved vegetable water and bring slowly to the boil. Add the vegetable extract, bay leaf, and salt and pepper and simmer for 5 minutes.
3. Arrange the vegetables in a large buttered ovenproof dish and pour over the sauce, discarding the bay leaf.
4. To make the crumble, mix the flour and oats together, rub in the butter, then stir in remaining ingredients.
5. Sprinkle over the vegetables and cook in a preheated oven, 200°C/400°F/Gas Mark 6, for 30 minutes, until bubbling. Garnish with bay leaves and serve with a salad.

TOMATO TUMBLE

25 g (1 oz) butter
1 onion, sliced
1 red pepper, cored, seeded and diced
250 g (8 oz) mushrooms, sliced
500 g (1 lb) tomatoes, skinned and sliced
2 tablespoons tomato purée
2 teaspoons Worcestershire sauce
2 tablespoons chopped parsley
125 g (4 oz) Cheddar cheese, grated
salt and pepper to taste

FOR THE SCONE DOUGH:
250 g (8 oz) self-raising flour
1 teaspoon dried basil
pinch of salt
75 g (3 oz) butter
about 6 tablespoons milk

1. Melt the butter in a pan, add the onion and red pepper and sauté until the onion is transparent. Add the mushrooms and cook for 5 minutes.
2. Add the remaining ingredients, except the cheese, bring to the boil, then simmer for 5 minutes. Transfer to an ovenproof serving dish.
3. To make the scone dough, sift the flour into a bowl, add the basil and salt, then rub in the butter until the mixture resembles fine crumbs. Mix to a firm dough with the milk.
4. Roll out the dough on a lightly floured surface to a 2 cm (¾ inch) thickness and cut out twelve 5 cm (2 inch) rounds with a plain cutter.
5. Arrange the rounds on top of the tomato mixture and sprinkle with the cheese. Cook in a preheated oven, 220°C/425°F/Gas Mark 7, for about 20 minutes, until risen and golden brown. Serve with a crisp green vegetable.

Serves 4
Preparation time:
25 minutes
Cooking time:
About 20 minutes
Freezing:
Not recommended

BRUSSELS SPROUTS BRIGOULE

25 g (1 oz) butter
6 celery sticks, cut into matchstick pieces
2 carrots, cut into matchstick pieces
1 onion, sliced
500 g (1 lb) Brussels sprouts
1 tablespoon lemon juice
300 ml (½ pint) vegetable stock
439 g (15½ oz) can chestnuts, drained
salt and pepper to taste
chopped parsley to garnish

Serves 4
Preparation time:
20 minutes
Cooking time:
25–30 minutes
Freezing:
Not recommended

1. Melt the butter in a pan, add the celery, carrots, and onion and sauté for 15 minutes.
2. Add the Brussels sprouts, lemon juice and stock. Cover and simmer for 10–15 minutes, until the sprouts are tender. Add the chestnuts and heat through.
3. Season with salt and pepper, and sprinkle with parsley to serve.

STIR-FRIED CARROTS WITH ORANGE

The natural sweetness of carrots is subtly flavoured with orange and mustard.

500 g (1 lb) even-size carrots
2 tablespoons oil
1 small onion, chopped
grated rind and juice of 1 large orange
1 tablespoon coarse-grain mustard
salt and pepper to taste
parsley or carrot tops to garnish

Serves 4
Preparation time:
15 minutes
Cooking time:
10 minutes
Freezing:
Not recommended

1. Cut the carrots into matchstick pieces, about 5 cm (2 inches) long and 5 mm (¼ inch) thick.
2. Heat the oil in a large frying pan or wok, add the carrots and onion and sauté over high heat for 5 minutes.
3. Stir in the orange rind and juice, mustard, and salt and pepper and simmer gently for 4–5 minutes, until the orange juice is reduced to a syrupy glaze.
4. Garnish with parsley or carrot tops to serve.

BAKED RED CABBAGE

125 g (4 oz) dried chestnuts, or 250 g (8 oz) fresh chestnuts, shelled
1 red cabbage, shredded
25 g (1 oz) butter
1 large onion, sliced
1 large cooking apple, peeled, cored and sliced
3 tablespoons red wine vinegar
1 tablespoon dark brown soft sugar
8 juniper berries, crushed
150 ml (1/4 pint) vegetable stock
1 tablespoon cornflour
salt and pepper to taste

Serves 4–6
Preparation time: 20 minutes, plus soaking time
Cooking time: About 1½ hours
Freezing: Recommended

1. If using dried chestnuts, cover with cold water, bring to the boil, then simmer for 5 minutes. Leave overnight to swell. Drain, reserving 3 tablespoons of the water.
2. Cover the cabbage with boiling water, then drain thoroughly.
3. Melt the butter in a pan, add the onion and sauté until transparent.
4. Arrange the cabbage, chestnuts, onion and apple in layers in a large flameproof casserole. Sprinkle with the vinegar, sugar, juniper berries and the reserved liquid. Cover and cook in a preheated oven, 160°C/325°F/Gas Mark 3, for about 1½ hours, until tender.
5. Gradually mix the stock into the cornflour, then stir into the casserole. Return to the oven, or simmer on top of the stove, stirring, until thickened. Season with salt and pepper. Serve immediately.

VARIATION

Add 125 g (4 oz) seedless grapes with the stock at stage 5.

JERUSALEM CHIPS

Quite simply chips made from Jerusalem artichokes.

750 g (1½ lb) large Jerusalem artichokes
oil for deep-frying
salt to taste
chopped parsley and chives to garnish

Serves 4
Preparation time: 20 minutes
Cooking time: 4–5 minutes
Freezing: Not recommended

1. Scrub the artichokes well; peel only if necessary. Cut into medium-size chips.
2. Heat the oil in a large wide pan and deep-fry the chips, stirring occasionally, until golden brown.
3. Drain on kitchen paper, then sprinkle with salt and the parsley and chives. Serve immediately.

CRISPY FRIED OKRA

It is essential that the okra is sliced as thinly as possible and the oil is very hot. Cook in two batches, if necessary.

500 g (1 lb) okra, sliced very thinly
1 teaspoon turmeric
2 teaspoons paprika
½ teaspoon salt
6 tablespoons oil
1 teaspoon mustard seeds
lemon slices and parsley sprigs to garnish

1. Toss the okra with the turmeric, paprika and salt until evenly coated.
2. Heat the oil with the mustard seeds in a very large frying pan until the seeds pop.
3. Add the okra and cook over a high heat until crisp. Serve immediately, garnished with lemon and parsley.

Serves 4
Preparation time:
20 minutes
Cooking time:
About 5 minutes
Freezing:
Not recommended

BAKED SWEET POTATOES WITH RUM AND MARMALADE GLAZE

Sweet potatoes have a distinctive flavour which goes so well with sweet spices.

750 g (1½ lb) sweet potatoes, cut into 2.5 cm (1 inch) chunks
4 tablespoons dark rum
4 tablespoons coarse-cut orange marmalade
4 tablespoons sunflower or pumpkin seeds
grated rind and juice of 1 large orange
25 g (1 oz) butter
1 teaspoon ground ginger
½ teaspoon ground allspice
½ teaspoon ground cinnamon
¼ teaspoon ground mace
salt and pepper to taste

Serves 4
Preparation time:
15 minutes
Cooking time:
45 minutes
Freezing:
Not recommended

1. Place all the ingredients in a flameproof casserole and mix well. Cover and cook in a preheated oven, 200°C/ 400°F/Gas Mark 6, for 45 minutes, until just tender.
2. Place on top of the stove, remove the lid and bubble until the juices become a thick glaze. Serve immediately.

ASPARAGUS QUILLS WITH PARMESAN AND WALNUTS

Fresh asparagus is truly delicious—extra special if prepared this way.

750 g (1½ lb) asparagus spears
25 g (1 oz) butter
50 g (2 oz) walnut pieces, chopped roughly
4 tablespoons double cream
40 g (1½ oz) Parmesan cheese, grated
salt and pepper to taste

Serves 4
Preparation time:
20 minutes
Cooking time:
About 10 minutes
Freezing:
Not recommended

1. Cut off the tough woody ends from the asparagus, then either carefully peel the stalks or, with a small sharp knife, remove the scaly leaf points.
2. Cut the asparagus diagonally into 7.5 cm (3 inch) lengths and steam or cook in boiling water for 3–5 minutes, until just tender. Drain well.
3. Arrange in a heatproof serving dish. Dot with the butter, sprinkle with the walnuts, and salt and pepper, and spoon the cream on top. Sprinkle with the cheese and place under a preheated hot grill for about 5 minutes, until golden and bubbling. Serve immediately.

SURPRISE POTATO CAKES

The surprise is the spiced hazelnut centre. The coconut coating gives a good contrast of texture.

25 g (1 oz) butter
125 g (4 oz) onion, chopped finely
50 g (2 oz) hazelnuts, chopped
1 teaspoon cumin seeds
½ teaspoon turmeric
½ green pepper, cored, seeded and chopped finely
1 tablespoon tomato purée
2 tomatoes, skinned and chopped
squeeze of lemon juice
1 kg (2 lb) potatoes, boiled and well drained
1 egg, separated
50–75 g (2–3 oz) desiccated coconut
salt and pepper to taste
lemon slices and parsley sprigs to garnish

Serves 4
Preparation time: 35 minutes
Cooking time: 20–25 minutes
Freezing: Recommended

1. Melt the butter in a pan, add the onion, hazelnuts and cumin seeds and sauté until golden. Stir in the turmeric, green pepper, tomato purée, tomatoes and lemon juice. Cook, stirring occasionally, until fairly dry, then leave to cool.
2. Mash the potatoes with the egg yolk, and salt and pepper. Using floured hands, shape into 8 cakes. Spoon one eighth of the filling onto each cake, then work the potato around the filling to encase it.
3. Dip each cake into the lightly beaten egg white, then into the coconut. Place on a greased baking sheet and cook in a preheated oven, 220°C/425°F/Gas Mark 7, for 20–25 minutes, until golden brown. Garnish with lemon and parsley and serve with a crisp green vegetable or salad.

BEETROOT NESTS

These attractive 'nests' can be topped with soured cream and sprinkled with extra chives before serving if you prefer.

1 kg (2 lb) potatoes
125 g (4 oz) Cheddar cheese, grated
1 tablespoon horseradish mustard
2 tablespoons milk
25 g (1 oz) butter
1 onion, diced
250 g (8 oz) cooked beetroot, diced
2 tablespoons wine vinegar
1 tablespoon snipped chives
salt and pepper to taste

1. Steam or cook the potatoes in boiling salted water for about 20 minutes, until tender. Drain well. Add the cheese, mustard, milk, and salt and pepper and mash well. Leave to cool.
2. Place the potato in a large piping bag fitted with a star nozzle and pipe 4 large 'nests' on a greased baking sheet. Place under a preheated hot grill for 5 minutes, until golden. Keep warm.
3. Melt the butter in a pan, add the onion and sauté until transparent. Stir in the beetroot and sauté for 2–3 minutes. Add the vinegar and bubble gently. Stir in the chives, and salt and pepper.
4. Spoon the beetroot into the potato nests and serve immediately.

Serves 4
Preparation time:
25 minutes
Cooking time:
25–30 minutes
Freezing:
Not recommended

BROAD BEANS WITH LEMON AND SESAME SEED SAUCE

500 g (1 lb) shelled fresh or frozen broad beans
25 g (1 oz) butter
1 onion, chopped finely
350 g (12 oz) tomatoes, chopped
4 tablespoons sesame seeds
grated rind and juice of ½ lemon
142 ml (5 fl oz) carton soured cream
salt and pepper to taste
tomato, lemon slices and parsley to garnish

Serves 4
Preparation time: 15 minutes
Cooking time: About 10 minutes
Freezing: Not recommended

1. Steam or cook the broad beans in the minimum of boiling water for 5–7 minutes, until just tender. Drain and set aside.
2. Melt the butter in a pan, add the onion and sauté until transparent. Add the beans, tomatoes and sesame seeds and cook, stirring, for 1–2 minutes.
3. Stir in the lemon rind and juice, soured cream, and salt and pepper and heat through gently. Serve hot, garnished with tomato, lemon and parsley.

TURNIP WITH APPLE AND PORT

Turnip is one of the most under-rated of all vegetables—give it a try this way.

750 g (1½ lb) young turnips
15 g (½ oz) butter
1 tablespoon oil
2 large Cox's Orange Pippin apples, cored and sliced thickly
4 tablespoons port
8 sage leaves, shredded
salt and pepper to taste
sage leaves to garnish

Serves 4
Preparation time: 15 minutes
Cooking time: About 15 minutes
Freezing: Not recommended

1. Peel the turnips if necessary, then halve if large. Steam or cook in boiling water for 5–7 minutes, until almost tender. Drain.
2. Heat the butter and oil in a large frying pan or wok, add the turnips and sauté lightly. Add the apples and sauté for 1–2 minutes.
3. Add the port, sage, and salt and pepper. Allow the mixture to bubble rapidly to reduce the port to a syrupy glaze.
4. Serve immediately, garnished with sage leaves.

SWEET AND SOUR CABBAGE

2 tablespoons oil
1 onion, sliced thinly
175 g (6 oz) carrots, sliced thinly
500 g (1 lb) green or white cabbage, shredded finely
3 tablespoons clear honey
3 tablespoons cider vinegar
1 teaspoon cornflour
1 teaspoon grated fresh root ginger
50 g (2 oz) unsalted peanuts, cashews or almonds, toasted
salt and pepper to taste

1. Heat the oil in a large frying pan or wok, add the onion and carrots and sauté for 3 minutes over a high heat. Add the cabbage and sauté for 5 minutes.
2. Mix together the honey, vinegar, cornflour and ginger and pour over the vegetables. Stir well and simmer for 5 minutes.
3. Season with salt and pepper, then sprinkle with the nuts. Serve immediately.

Serves 4
Preparation time: 20 minutes
Cooking time: 13 minutes
Freezing: Not recommended

MAPLEWOOD LATKES WITH APPLE SAUCE

This recipe comes from a friend in New Jersey. It is quick to prepare in a food processor—if you don't have one, grate the potato instead.

1 egg
1 small onion, chopped
2 tablespoons plain flour
½ teaspoon salt
good pinch of pepper
3 potatoes, weighing about 500 g (1 lb), chopped roughly
6 tablespoons oil

FOR THE APPLE SAUCE:
500 g (1 lb) cooking apples, peeled, cored and chopped
25 g (1 oz) light brown soft sugar
2 tablespoons water
2 cloves
TO SERVE (OPTIONAL):
soured cream
snipped chives

Serves 4
Preparation time: 15 minutes
Cooking time: 5–6 minutes per batch
Freezing: Recommended

1. Place the egg, onion, flour, salt and pepper in a food processor and work together to a purée. Add the potatoes and work until fairly smooth.
2. Heat about one third of the oil in a large non-stick frying pan. Pour 3–4 tablespoons of the mixture into the pan and flatten slightly to a 10 cm (4 inch) round. Repeat twice more to cook three latkes at a time.
3. Cook for about 3 minutes on each side until crisp and golden. Drain on kitchen paper and keep warm while cooking the rest, adding a little more oil when necessary.
4. To make the apple sauce, place all the ingredients in a saucepan, cover and simmer for about 10 minutes, until soft and pulpy. Remove the cloves and beat well with a wooden spoon.
5. Serve the latkes hot with the warm or cold apple sauce, and soured cream sprinkled with chives, if you wish.

CAULIFLOWER CHEESE FRITTERS

250 g (8 oz) cauliflower florets
50 g (2 oz) butter
75 g (3 oz) plain flour
pinch of mustard powder
300 ml (½ pint) milk
25 g (1 oz) spring onions, chopped
50 g (2 oz) matured Cheddar cheese, grated
1 egg, beaten
50 g (2 oz) dried breadcrumbs
salt and pepper to taste
oil for deep-frying
tomato wedges to garnish

1. Steam or cook the cauliflower in boiling water for 5–7 minutes, until just tender. Drain well, then chop roughly.
2. Melt the butter in a pan, stir in 50 g (2 oz) of the flour and the mustard and cook for 1–2 minutes.
3. Gradually stir in the milk, then cook, stirring, for 1–2 minutes until thickened. Remove from the heat and beat in the spring onions and cheese, then add the cauliflower, and salt and pepper. Leave until cold.
4. Divide the mixture into 12 portions. Coat with the remaining flour, dip in the beaten egg, then into the breadcrumbs.
5. Heat the oil in a large pan and deep-fry the fritters until golden brown. Drain on kitchen paper and serve immediately garnished with tomato wedges.

Serves 4
Preparation time:
30 minutes
Cooking time:
30 minutes
Freezing:
Recommended

ORIENTAL SALAD

There is no substitute for the wonderful flavour of fresh coconut. If you wish, soak the bean sprouts in iced water for 5–10 minutes to improve their crispness; drain well.

350 g (12 oz) bean sprouts
125 g (4 oz) fresh coconut, grated coarsely
2 large carrots, grated coarsely
FOR THE DRESSING:
juice of 2 limes or 1 large lemon
4 tablespoons sunflower oil
50 g (2 oz) stem ginger, chopped
2 tablespoons sesame seeds
2 tablespoons light soy sauce
salt and pepper to taste

Serves 4–6
Preparation time:
30 minutes
Freezing:
Not recommended

1. Combine the bean sprouts, coconut and carrots in a salad bowl.
2. Place the dressing ingredients in a screw-top jar and shake well. Pour over the salad and toss well.

GINGER AND BROCCOLI SALAD

Broccoli is rarely used in salads, but it is delicious with this oriental flavouring.

2 tablespoons clear honey (preferably acacia)
2 tablespoons oil
2 tablespoons soy sauce
1½ teaspoons finely grated root ginger
1 clove garlic, crushed
50 g (2 oz) cocktail onions
750 g (1½ lb) broccoli
50 g (2 oz) blanched almonds, toasted

Serves 4
Preparation time:
15 minutes
Cooking time:
5–7 minutes
Freezing:
Not recommended

1. Place the honey, oil, soy sauce, ginger and garlic in a large bowl and mix well. Add the cocktail onions.
2. Remove the coarse outer skin from the broccoli stalks, then cut the stalks into 2.5 cm (1 inch) pieces.
3. Steam the broccoli florets and stalks for 5–7 minutes until just tender but still crisp. Add to the honey mixture, toss well and leave until cold, stirring well occasionally.
4. Stir in toasted almonds just before serving.

CAULIFLOWER SALAD

Raw cauliflower has a good crunchy texture and goes well with dates, banana and orange in this unusual salad.

1 cauliflower, weighing about 350–400 g (12–14 oz)
50 g (2 oz) stoned dates, chopped
50 g (2 oz) walnuts, chopped
2 bananas, sliced
grated rind and juice of 1 small orange
1 tablespoon lemon juice
6 tablespoons Mayonnaise (page 71)
salt and pepper to taste
orange slices and parsley to garnish

Serves 4
Preparation time:
20 minutes
Freezing:
Not recommended

1. Cut the cauliflower into tiny florets and dice the stalks. Mix with the dates, walnuts and bananas in a salad bowl.
2. Mix the remaining ingredients together, pour over the salad and toss well.
3. Serve immediately, garnished with orange slices and parsley, as part of a salad selection.

MIDDLE EASTERN SALAD

A spinach salad containing some warm ingredients—sautéed onion rings and mushroom slices—tossed in a tangy yogurt dressing.

125 g (4 oz) red lentils
500 g (1 lb) spinach
2 carrots
1 tablespoon oil
15 g (½ oz) butter
250 g (8 oz) onions, cut into rings
250 g (8 oz) mushrooms, sliced
2 tablespoons French Dressing (page 70)
6 tablespoons natural yogurt
salt and pepper to taste

Serves 4–6
Preparation time:
30 minutes
Cooking time:
10–15 minutes
Freezing:
Not recommended

1. Cook the lentils in about 300 ml (½ pint) water for 10–15 minutes, until just tender and all the liquid has been absorbed.
2. Remove the stems from the spinach; shred coarsely.
3. Using a potato peeler, shave the carrots into ribbons.
4. Heat the oil and butter in a pan, add the onions and mushrooms and sauté until golden.
5. Mix the French dressing and yogurt together.
6. Place all the ingredients in a salad bowl and toss well. Serve immediately, as a main course salad or as part of a salad selection.

CRUNCHY POTATO SALAD

750 g ($1\frac{1}{2}$ lb) new potatoes
2 celery sticks, chopped
8 radishes, sliced
50 g (2 oz) dill pickle, chopped
2 large spring onions, sliced
4 tablespoons chopped parsley
50 g (2 oz) salted peanuts
FOR THE DRESSING:
4 tablespoons soured cream
4 tablespoons Mayonnaise (page 71)
1 tablespoon wine vinegar
salt and pepper to taste

1. Cook the potatoes in boiling salted water until just tender; drain. Cool, then chop roughly if you wish. Place in a salad bowl and add the remaining ingredients.
2. Stir the dressing ingredients together, add to the salad and toss well.

Serves 4
Preparation time: 20 minutes
Freezing: Not recommended

WATERCRESS, PEAR AND PECAN SALAD

A lovely mix of colour, flavour and texture. The dressing will keep for several days in the refrigerator.

1 bunch watercress
1 head chicory, sliced
2 large oranges, segmented
2 ripe pears, sliced thinly
50 g (2 oz) pecan nuts, toasted

FOR THE DRESSING:
1 large egg (size 1)
2 tablespoons caster sugar
3 tablespoons white wine vinegar
1 teaspoon dried tarragon
6 tablespoons double cream

Serves 4
Preparation time:
About 30 minutes
Freezing:
Not recommended

1. First make the dressing. Beat the egg and sugar together in a heatproof bowl, then add the vinegar and tarragon. Place over a pan of simmering water and cook, stirring, until thickened. Leave until cold, then stir in the cream.
2. Place the watercress and chicory in a salad bowl and mix well. Add the oranges, pears and pecans.
3. Serve the salad accompanied by the dressing.

SWEET AND SOUR AUBERGINE SALAD

Salting the aubergines helps to remove any bitterness.

500 g (1 lb) aubergines, sliced
4 tablespoons olive oil
250 g (8 oz) onions, sliced
2 cloves garlic, crushed
25 g (1 oz) demerara sugar
25 g (1 oz) raisins
juice of 2 lemons
2 red peppers, cored, seeded and quartered
salt and pepper to taste
chopped parsley to garnish

Serves 4–6
Preparation time:
25 minutes
Cooking time:
15 minutes
Freezing:
Not recommended

1. Sprinkle the aubergines with salt and set aside.
2. Heat the oil in a pan, add the onions and garlic and sauté until transparent.
3. Rinse and dry the aubergines and add to the pan. Cover and cook for 10 minutes, stirring occasionally.
4. Add the sugar, raisins and lemon juice and bring back to a simmer. Remove from the heat, transfer to a salad bowl and leave until cold.
5. Grill the pepper quarters, skin side up, until charred and blistered, then remove the skin. Cut the pepper into strips and add to the salad with salt and pepper. Stir well and sprinkle with parsley to serve.

AMERICAN COURGETTE SALAD

A crunchy green salad with a sweet and sour tang—leave it to marinate for as long as possible.

500 g (1 lb) small courgettes, sliced
6 celery sticks, sliced
1 green pepper, cored, seeded and diced
2 spring onions, sliced
125 g (4 oz) green grapes, halved and seeds removed if necessary

FOR THE DRESSING:
4 tablespoons cider vinegar
2 tablespoons olive oil
1 tablespoon light brown soft sugar
salt and pepper to taste

Serves 4–6
Preparation time:
30 minutes
Freezing:
Not recommended

1. Place the courgettes, celery, green pepper and spring onions in a salad bowl.
2. Mix the dressing ingredients together and add to the salad. Mix well, cover and leave until required.
3. Add the grapes and toss gently to serve.

FRUITED TABBOULEH WITH COURGETTES

My version of a well-known Middle Eastern salad.

250 g (8 oz) bulgar wheat
6 tablespoons olive oil
juice of 1 lemon
2 tablespoons chopped coriander
3 tablespoons each chopped mint and chives
1 clove garlic, crushed
250 g (8 oz) small courgettes, sliced thinly lengthways
50 g (2 oz) dried apricots
25 g (1 oz) currants
salt and pepper to taste

Serves 6
Preparation time:
About 35 minutes
Freezing:
Not recommended

1. Wash the bulgar wheat well, then leave to soak for about 30 minutes in cold water to come about 2.5 cm (1 inch) above the level of the wheat. Drain well and squeeze out excess moisture by placing the grain in a clean tea towel.
2. Combine with the remaining ingredients in a large bowl. Toss well and leave in a cool place for the flavours to develop.
3. Toss well again before serving.

CRUNCHY GREEN SALAD

125 g (4 oz) mixed green salad leaves, such as frisé, lambs' lettuce, iceberg lettuce
1 carton mustard and cress
50 g (2 oz) celery, sliced
50 g (2 oz) leek or spring onions, sliced
125 g (4 oz) courgette or cucumber, sliced
1 crisp green eating apple, diced
1 ripe avocado, diced
6 tablespoons chopped herbs
4–6 tablespoons French Dressing (page 70)

Mix all the salad ingredients together in a large bowl. Toss with the dressing just before serving.

Serves 4–6
Preparation time:
25 minutes
Freezing:
Not recommended

SWEET AND SOUR RED SALAD

A brightly-coloured salad with an oriental flavour—a combination of all the reds.

250 g (8 oz) red cabbage, shredded
432 g (15 1/4 oz) can red kidney beans, drained
125 g (4 oz) radishes, sliced
1 small red onion, sliced very thinly
1 red pepper, cored, seeded and diced
200 g (7 oz) beetroot, cut into strips
FOR THE DRESSING:
4 tablespoons red wine vinegar
4 tablespoons light brown soft sugar
2 tablespoons light soy sauce
2 teaspoons oil

Serves 6
Preparation time:
35 minutes
Freezing:
Not recommended

1. Cover the cabbage with boiling water, leave for 5 minutes, then drain well.
2. Combine all the salad ingredients.
3. Combine all the dressing ingredients.
4. Mix the salad and dressing together and leave until required.

CURRIED PINEAPPLE AND AVOCADO SALAD

1 tablespoon oil
125 g (4 oz) onion, chopped finely
2 teaspoons curry powder
2 tomatoes, chopped
150 ml (1/4 pint) vegetable stock
4 tablespoons Mayonnaise (page 71)
4 tablespoons natural yogurt
1 pineapple
1 large avocado, diced
4 celery sticks, sliced
poppadums to serve

Serves 4–6
Preparation time:
25 minutes
Cooking time:
15–20 minutes
Freezing:
Not recommended

1. Heat the oil in a pan, add the onion and curry powder and sauté for 5 minutes.
2. Add the tomatoes and stock and boil rapidly for 10–15 minutes, until a thick paste forms. Leave until cold, then rub through a sieve. Stir in the mayonnaise and yogurt.
3. Cut the pineapple in half lengthways and carefully remove the flesh, leaving the shells intact. Dice the pineapple and add to the sauce with the avocado and celery. Mix carefully, then pile into the pineapple shells. Serve with poppadums.

MARINATED BEAN SALAD

250 g (8 oz) dried haricot beans, soaked overnight
125 g (4 oz) leeks, sliced thinly
2 large celery sticks, sliced
250 g (8 oz) cherry tomatoes, halved
1 small red pepper, cored, seeded and diced
4 tablespoons chopped mixed herbs, e.g. marjoram, parsley

FOR THE DRESSING:
6 tablespoons olive oil
3 tablespoons lemon juice
grated rind of 1 lemon
1 tablespoon coarse-grain mustard
1 clove garlic, crushed
salt and pepper to taste

Serves 4–6
Preparation time: 30 minutes, plus soaking time
Cooking time: About 1 hour
Freezing: Not recommended

1. Drain the beans, cover with fresh cold water and bring to the boil. Boil briskly for 10 minutes, then cover and simmer for about 40 minutes, until tender. Drain well.
2. Mix the dressing ingredients together. Add the beans and leave until cold.
3. Add the remaining ingredients and toss well.
4. Serve as part of a salad selection, or add diced cheese or hard-boiled egg to make a main course meal.

TOMATO SALAD WITH HERB SAUCE

There is nothing to compare with the simple combination of sun ripened tomatoes and cucumber. Use either thick Greek yogurt or soured cream, or a combination of the two, for the dressing.

500 g (1 lb) firm ripe tomatoes, sliced
175 g (6 oz) cucumber, sliced
mint sprigs to garnish
FOR THE DRESSING:
240 g (8 oz) carton Greek yogurt, or 250 ml (8 fl oz) soured cream
4 tablespoons chopped basil or mint
2 tablespoons chopped chives or spring onion
2 tablespoons French Dressing (page 70)
salt and pepper to taste
paprika to garnish

Serves 4–6
Preparation time: 15 minutes
Freezing: Not recommended

1. Arrange the tomatoes and cucumber on a serving platter and garnish with mint.
2. Mix the dressing ingredients together and spoon into a bowl. Sprinkle with the paprika.
3. Serve the salad accompanied by the dressing.

ITALIAN TORTELLONI SALAD

Fresh pasta shapes make this a substantial salad.

250 g (8.82 oz) packet spinach tortelloni
250 g (8 oz) button mushrooms, sliced
6 tablespoons French Dressing (page 70)
175 g (6 oz) cherry tomatoes, halved
175 g (6 oz) courgettes, cut into 2.5 cm (1 inch) sticks
6 spring onions, sliced

Serves 4
Preparation time:
About 30 minutes
Freezing:
Not recommended

Cook the tortelloni according to packet directions. Drain well and mix immediately with the mushrooms and dressing. Leave until cold, then stir in remaining ingredients.

SUNDAY NIGHT SALAD BOWL

1 kg (2 lb) potatoes, boiled
350 g (12 oz) assorted salad leaves, such as spinach, lettuce, frisé
4 celery sticks, cut into strips
125 g (4 oz) carrots, cut into strips
125 g (4 oz) cucumber, cut into strips
125 g (4 oz) radishes, sliced
4 spring onions, sliced
350 g (12 oz) cheese of your choice, sliced
12 quails eggs, hard-boiled and halved
4 tablespoons sesame seeds, toasted
FOR THE DRESSING:
300 ml (½ pint) Mayonnaise (page 71)
2 tablespoons wine vinegar
2 tablespoons each chopped parsley and tarragon
4 tablespoons chopped chives or spring onions

Serves 6
Preparation time:
35 minutes
Freezing:
Not recommended

1. Drain the potatoes well, cut into large dice and leave until cold.
2. Combine all the salad ingredients in one large salad bowl or 4 individual ones.
3. Mix the dressing ingredients together. Pour over the salad and toss well just before serving.
4. Serve with hot bread for a complete meal.

MIXED BEAN SALAD

A simple yet delicious combination of beans and hazelnuts in a garlic and lemon dressing.

350 g (12 oz) green beans, cut into 5 cm (2 inch) lengths
432 g (15¼ oz) can chick peas, drained
432 g (15¼ oz) can red kidney beans, drained
75 g (3 oz) hazelnuts, chopped and toasted
FOR THE DRESSING:
4 tablespoons olive oil
grated rind of ½ lemon
2 tablespoons lemon juice
1–2 cloves garlic, crushed
salt and pepper to taste

Serves 4
Preparation time:
20 minutes
Freezing:
Not recommended

1. Steam or cook the green beans in boiling salted water for 5 minutes. Drain and leave until cold.
2. Place in a salad bowl with the chick peas, kidney beans and hazelnuts.
3. Put the dressing ingredients in a screw-top jar and shake. Pour over the salad and toss just before serving.

CURRIED MELON AND BEAN SALAD

I like to mix fruit and vegetables in salads. This combination marries well with the curry yogurt dressing.

432 g (15¼ oz) can borlotti beans, drained
6 large celery sticks, sliced
1 melon, weighing about 750 g (1½ lb), diced
4 spring onions, sliced
4 tablespoons Greek yogurt
4 tablespoons Mayonnaise (page 71)
1 tablespoon medium hot curry powder
salt to taste

1. Combine the beans, celery, melon and spring onions in a salad bowl.
2. Mix together the yogurt, mayonnaise and curry powder, add to the salad and season with salt.
3. Serve as part of a salad selection.

Serves 4
Preparation time:
20 minutes
Freezing:
Not recommended

SUE'S FRENCH SALAD

A fabulous combination of green salad vegetables in a garlicky dressing—substantial and nutritious enough to be a main course.

250 g (8 oz) French beans
250 g (8 oz) mangetouts
250 g (8 oz) iceberg lettuce, shredded
1 carton mustard and cress or bunch of watercress
8 spring onions, sliced
1 avocado, sliced
25 g (1 oz) pine nuts
2 cloves garlic, crushed
6 tablespoons French Dressing (below)
salt and pepper to taste

Serves 4–6
Preparation time:
30 minutes
Freezing:
Not recommended

1. Cook the beans in boiling water for 2 minutes. Add the mangetouts and cook for 1 minute. Drain and cool quickly in iced water. Drain well.
2. Place all the ingredients in a salad bowl and toss well.
3. Serve immediately, with crusty bread or as part of a salad selection.

CELERIAC, WALNUT AND APPLE SALAD

1 celeriac, weighing about 1 kg (2 lb)
4 tablespoons cider vinegar
200 ml (1/3 pint) Mayonnaise (opposite)
3 crisp eating apples, sliced
50 g (2 oz) walnuts, chopped roughly
salt and pepper to taste

Serves 6
Preparation time:
25 minutes
Freezing:
Not recommended

1. Grate the celeriac coarsely and mix with the vinegar and mayonnaise in a salad bowl.
2. Add the apples and walnuts just before serving. Toss well and season with salt and pepper.

FRENCH DRESSING

2 tablespoons wine vinegar
3–4 tablespoons sunflower oil
3–4 tablespoons olive oil
1 teaspoon French mustard (preferably coarse-grain)
salt, pepper and sugar to taste

Makes about 250 ml (8 fl oz)
Preparation time:
5 minutes
Freezing:
Not recommended

Place all the ingredients in a screw-top jar, seasoning with salt, pepper and sugar to taste, and shake well to mix.

MAYONNAISE

2 large egg yolks (size 1 or 2)
½ teaspoon mustard powder
300 ml (½ pint) oil
1 tablespoon white wine vinegar or lemon juice
salt and pepper to taste

1. Place the egg yolks, mustard and salt and pepper in an electric blender or food processor and work until smooth.
2. With the machine running, pour in the oil slowly in a steady stream, until the mixture is thick and creamy.
3. Add the vinegar or lemon juice and blend for a few seconds. Check the seasoning.

Makes about 300 ml (½ pint)
Preparation time:
10–15 minutes
Freezing:
Not recommended

CARIBBEAN CALALOO SOUP

Based on a delicious soup I tasted in the Caribbean. Locals use calaloo leaves; I've substituted spinach. When pumpkin is out of season, use squash instead.

25 g (1 oz) butter
4 cloves garlic, sliced thinly
250 g (8 oz) spinach, shredded finely
250 g (8 oz) wedge of pumpkin, diced
2 potatoes, diced
1.2 litres (2 pints) vegetable stock
salt and pepper to taste

Serves 4
Preparation time: 15 minutes
Cooking time: About 15 minutes
Freezing: Recommended

1. Melt the butter in a pan, add the garlic and sauté until golden. Stir in the spinach and cook for 1–2 minutes, until bright green.
2. Add the remaining ingredients, cover and simmer for about 15 minutes, until the vegetables are tender.

CAULIFLOWER AND COCONUT SOUP

Creamed coconut marries well with the spicy flavours in this soup; it may be chopped or grated to melt more easily.

2 tablespoons oil
1 onion, chopped finely
1 large carrot, diced
250 g (8 oz) cauliflower florets
1 cooking apple, peeled, cored and diced
½ teaspoon each ground cumin, coriander, turmeric and ginger
¼ teaspoon chilli powder
1 litre (1¾ pints) vegetable stock
50 g (2 oz) creamed coconut
3 tablespoons chopped coriander leaves
432 g (15¼ oz) can borlotti beans, drained
salt and pepper to taste

Serves 4–6
Preparation time: 15 minutes
Cooking time: About 25 minutes
Freezing: Recommended

1. Heat the oil in a pan, add the onion and carrot and sauté for 5 minutes. Add the cauliflower, apple and spices, stir well and cook for 1–2 minutes.
2. Add the stock, bring to the boil, then cover and simmer for 20 minutes.
3. Stir in the remaining ingredients and simmer gently until the creamed coconut has melted. Serve hot.

CLASSIC MINESTRONE

25 g (1 oz) butter
3 tablespoons olive oil
1 very large onion, chopped
2 carrots, diced
1 potato, diced
125 g (4 oz) shelled fresh or frozen broad beans
1 large courgette, diced
50 g (2 oz) green beans, cut into 2.5 cm (1 inch) pieces
125 g (4 oz) green cabbage, shredded
125 g (4 oz) broccoli or cauliflower, cut into florets
397 g (14 oz) can peeled tomatoes
1.2 litres (2 pints) vegetable stock
50 g (2 oz) spaghetti, broken into short lengths
salt and pepper to taste
grated Parmesan cheese to serve

Serves 4–6
Preparation time:
20 minutes
Cooking time:
About 30 minutes
Freezing:
Recommended

1. Heat the butter and oil in a large saucepan, add the onion and sauté until transparent.
2. Add each vegetable in order; stir well between each addition and cook each one for about 1 minute before adding the next.
3. Add the tomatoes with their juice and the stock and bring to the boil. Add the spaghetti and simmer for about 20 minutes. Season with salt and pepper.
4. Serve with Parmesan cheese and crusty bread.

ITALIAN PEASANT SOUP

25 g (1 oz) butter
1 onion, chopped
350 g (12 oz) white cabbage, shredded finely
50 g (2 oz) Italian risotto rice
1.2 litres (2 pints) vegetable stock
1 large rosemary sprig
1 large thyme sprig
1 bay leaf
50 g (2 oz) Parmesan cheese, grated
salt and pepper to taste

Serves 4
Preparation time:
15 minutes
Cooking time:
30 minutes
Freezing:
Recommended at end of stage 2

1. Melt the butter in a pan, add the onion and cabbage and sauté for 5 minutes, stirring frequently.
2. Add the rice and stock and bring to the boil. Add the herbs, cover and simmer for 30 minutes. Remove the herb stalks and bay leaf.
3. Stir in the Parmesan cheese, and salt and pepper.
4. Serve with crusty bread.

HOT AND SOUR SOUP

Hot and sour soup has always been one of my favourite warming winter soups—this all vegetable variation is delicious.

25 g (1 oz) dried Chinese mushrooms, or 50 g (2 oz) button mushrooms, sliced
25 g (1 oz) spring onions, sliced
25 g (1 oz) bamboo shoots, cut into matchstick pieces
25 g (1 oz) Chinese leaves, shredded finely
50 g (2 oz) frozen peas
25 g (1 oz) tofu, cut into matchstick pieces
1–2 small red chillies, seeded and sliced
900 ml (1½ pints) well flavoured vegetable stock
2 tablespoons light soy sauce
3 tablespoons wine vinegar
2 teaspoons cornflour
1 egg, beaten

Serves 4
Preparation time:
20 minutes
Cooking time:
5 minutes
Freezing:
Not recommended

1. Soak the dried mushrooms, if using, in boiling water while you prepare all the other vegetables. Drain, discard the stalks and slice the caps thinly.
2. Place all the vegetables, stock, soy sauce and vinegar in a saucepan and simmer gently for 3 minutes.
3. Blend the cornflour with a little water and add to the pan. Bring to the boil, stirring, then reduce heat to a simmer.
4. Pour the beaten egg through the prongs of a fork into the soup. Stir well, then serve immediately.

PURÉE OF WHITE BEAN SOUP WITH LEMON HERB BUTTER

250 g (8 oz) dried haricot beans, soaked overnight and drained
1 large onion, chopped
2 cloves garlic, chopped
1 bay leaf
few parsley sprigs
1.2 litres (2 pints) vegetable stock
salt and pepper to taste
FOR THE LEMON HERB BUTTER:
50 g (2 oz) butter, softened
grated rind of 1 lemon
1 tablespoon chopped thyme
1 clove garlic, crushed

1. Put the haricot beans into a large pan of boiling water and boil steadily for 10 minutes. Drain, then return the

beans to the pan. Add the remaining soup ingredients, bring to the boil, then cover and simmer for 1½–2 hours, until the beans are tender.

2. Meanwhile, make the lemon herb butter. Mix the ingredients together, place on foil or greaseproof paper and shape into a roll. Wrap in the foil or paper and chill until required.

3. Discard the bay leaf and purée the soup in a blender or food processor. Thin with a little extra stock or milk and heat through.

4. Transfer to warmed individual soup plates. Slice the herb butter thinly and add to the soup just before serving.

Serves 4
Preparation time:
20 minutes, plus soaking time
Cooking time:
1½–2 hours
Freezing:
Recommended

MUSHROOM AND WHEAT BERRY SOUP

A mushroom broth, made more substantial by the addition of wheat berries. If you have difficulty finding wheat berries, use green lentils instead.

175 g (6 oz) wheat berries
50 g (2 oz) butter
1 large onion, chopped
2 cloves garlic, chopped finely
250 g (8 oz) mushrooms, chopped finely
2 tablespoons coarse-grain mustard
1 teaspoon dried dill
1 teaspoon dried thyme
2 vegetable stock cubes
yeast extract or vegetable extract to taste

Serves 4–6
Preparation time:
15 minutes, plus soaking time
Cooking time:
About 45 minutes
Freezing:
Recommended

1. Soak the wheat berries in 1.5 litres (2½ pints) boiling water for at least 2 hours or overnight.
2. Melt the butter in a pan, add the onion, garlic and mushrooms and sauté for 10 minutes.
3. Add the wheat berries with their soaking water, and the remaining ingredients.
4. Bring to the boil, then cover and simmer for about 45 minutes, until the wheat is tender. Serve hot.

HAMPSHIRE WATERCRESS SOUP

25 g (1 oz) butter
250 g (8 oz) carrots, chopped
200–250 g (6–8 oz) watercress
500 g (1 lb) potatoes, chopped
1.2 litres (2 pints) vegetable stock
150 ml (¼ pint) milk
salt and pepper to taste
TO GARNISH:
few watercress leaves
little grated carrot

Serves 4–6
Preparation time:
15 minutes
Cooking time:
20 minutes
Freezing:
Recommended

1. Melt the butter in a pan, add the carrots and sauté for about 5 minutes. Add the watercress and cook for 1–2 minutes.
2. Add the potatoes and stock, bring to the boil, then cover and simmer for 20 minutes, until the vegetables are tender.
3. Leave to cool slightly, then purée in a blender or food processor. Return to the pan, add the milk, and salt and pepper and heat through. Transfer to warmed individual soup plates and garnish with watercress and carrot. Serve with crusty bread.

INDEX

Photography by: Laurie Evans
Designed by: Sue Storey
Home economist: Jane Suthering
Stylist: Penny Markham
Illustration by: Linda Smith
Typeset by Rowland Phototypesetting Limited